AMAZING MILITARY MACHINES

MILITARY AIRCRAFT

by Mari Schuh

PEBBLE
a capstone imprint

Published by Pebble, an imprint of Capstone.
1710 Roe Crest Drive, North Mankato, Minnesota 56003
capstonepub.com

Library of Congress Cataloging-in-Publication Data
Names: Schuh, Mari C., 1975- author.
Title: Military aircraft / Mari Schuh.
Description: North Mankato, Minnesota : Pebble, 2022. | Series: Amazing military machines | Includes bibliographical references. | Audience: Ages 5-8 | Audience: Grades K-1 | Summary: "Militaries need fast and powerful machines in the air. Fighter jets, cargo planes, and other amazing aircraft zoom over land and water to get the job done!"— Provided by publisher.
Identifiers: LCCN 2021056916 (print) | LCCN 2021056917 (ebook) | ISBN 9781666350289 (hardcover) | ISBN 9781666350326 (paperback) | ISBN 9781666350364 (ebook pdf) | ISBN 9781666350449 (kindle edition)
Subjects: LCSH: Airplanes, Military—Juvenile literature.
Classification: LCC UG1240 .S366 2022 (print) | LCC UG1240 (ebook) | DDC 358.4/183—dc23/eng/20211123
LC record available at https://lccn.loc.gov/2021056916
LC ebook record available at https://lccn.loc.gov/2021056917

Image Credits

AP Photo: Aaron Favila, 17; Newscom: Abaca/Yuri Belinsky, 9; Shutterstock: Amawasri Pakdara, 20 (bottom right), Fra tta, 20 (top right), InsectWorld, 16, Joe Ravi, 11, Oleksandr Lysenko, 20 (left), Rick Parsons, 7, VanderWolf Images, 6; U.S. Air Force photo by Airman 1st Class Bryan Guthrie, 18, Airman 1st Class Heather Leveille, 19, Airman 1st Class Luis A. Ruiz-Vazquez, 14, Senior Airman Tiffany A. Emery, 13, Staff Sgt. Alexander Cook, 5, Tech. Sgt. Matthew Lotz, Cover, Airman 1st Class Bailee A. Darbasie, 15; U.S. Navy photo by Mass Communication Specialist 3rd Class Brooke Macchietto/Released, 10

The appearance of U.S. Department of Defense (DoD) visual information does not imply or constitute DoD endorsement.

Editorial Credits

Editor: Erika L. Shores; Designer: Dina Her; Media Researcher: Jo Miller; Production Specialist: Tori Abraham

All internet sites appearing in back matter were available and accurate when this book was sent to press.

Printed and bound in the USA. PO4882

TABLE OF CONTENTS

Words in **bold** are in the glossary.

AWESOME AIRCRAFT

Military aircraft are amazing machines. Fighter jets and spy planes are fast. **Cargo** planes carry lots of equipment. They are very powerful. These strong aircraft are busy around the world.

fighter jets

F-16 FIGHTING FALCON

The F-16 fighter jet is used in 25 countries. More than 4,500 of these jets fly in the sky.

The F-16 is very fast. It can fly more than 1,300 miles (2,092 kilometers) per hour. It can also change directions quickly.

The **cockpit** window looks like a bubble. This helps the pilot see all around.

MI-26

The Mi-26 is huge and powerful. It is the biggest airlift helicopter in the world. It is about as tall as a three-story building. The Mi-26 carries loads as heavy as 20 tons. When it uses a sling, it can carry airplanes.

The Mi-26 takes off and lands **vertically**. It doesn't need a runway. It can go where airplanes can't go.

DASSAULT RAFALE

This fighter jet is used in many ways. It is used on aircraft carriers. It is also used on land bases.

Two **engines** give the jet power. Its **radars** find targets quicker than other aircraft. Sensors find targets too. This fast jet tracks many targets at the same time.

F-22 RAPTOR

The F-22 Raptor is a **stealth** fighter jet. Its design makes it hard to spot. It can't be seen on radar.

Look! The wings have a triangle shape. They hold tanks full of fuel. This jet travels faster than the speed of sound. Zoom! It quickly changes directions.

U-2

As a spy plane, the U-2 gathers images and data. It flies on long missions. Its wings are long and narrow. They help it fly high in the sky for many hours. The U-2 flies 70,000 feet (21 km) above Earth.

The air high in the sky is different. So U-2 pilots wear a pressure suit. It keeps them safe. The suit is like an astronaut's suit.

C-130 HERCULES

The C-130 Hercules moves troops from place to place. It moves equipment too. It can carry two large battle tanks.

This big aircraft lands in tight spaces.
It also lands on rough ground. It is used
around the world.

The C-130 is also used as a flying hospital.
It helps people hurt by **natural disasters**.
The C-130 brings supplies to people in need.

F-35 LIGHTNING II

The F-35's engine is the world's most powerful fighter engine. It helps the jet fly faster than the speed of sound.

The visor of the pilot's helmet is like a computer screen. Pilots don't need to look at screens in the cockpit. Instead, they read data on the helmet's visor. The F-35 is one of the many amazing aircraft zooming through the sky.

MAKE YOUR OWN AIRPLANE

Aircraft are different shapes and sizes.

This paper airplane looks unusual.

But see how well it flies!

What You Need

- scissors
- construction paper
- tape
- straws

What You Do

1. Cut two strips of paper. Cut one strip longer and wider than the other strip.

2. Make a loop with each strip. Tape the ends of each strip together.

3. The big loop is the back of the airplane. Put tape on the straw. Then attach the straw to the big loop.

4. Next, tape the small loop to the front of the straw. Make sure the two loops line up.

5. Hold the straw so the small loop is forward and both loops are on top of the straw.

6. Now throw your airplane! How does it fly?

GLOSSARY

cargo (KAR-goh)—the goods carried by a ship, vehicle, or aircraft

cockpit (KOK-pit)—the area in the front of a plane where the pilot sits

engine (EN-juhn)—a machine that uses fuel to power a vehicle

natural disaster (NACH-ur-uhl di-ZAS-tuhr)—an earthquake, flood, storm, or other deadly event caused by nature

radar (RAY-dar)—a device that uses radio waves to track the location of objects

stealth (STELTH)—having the ability to move secretly, without being seen by radar

vertical (VUR-tuh-kuhl)—straight up and down

READ MORE

Bassier, Emma. *Military Aircraft*. Minneapolis: DiscoverRoo, an imprint of Pop!, 2020.

Lanier, Wendy Hinote. *Fighter Jets*. Lake Elmo, MN: Focus Readers, 2019.

Vonder Brink, Tracy. *The United States Air Force*. North Mankato, MN: Pebble, 2021.

INTERNET SITES

NASA: Airplanes: Parts of a Plane
grc.nasa.gov/WWW/K-12/UEET/StudentSite/airplanes.html

Wonderopolis: How Do Helicopters Work?
wonderopolis.org/wonder/how-do-helicopters-work

INDEX

ABOUT THE AUTHOR

Mari Schuh's love of reading began with cereal boxes at the kitchen table. Today, she is the author of hundreds of nonfiction books for beginning readers. Mari lives in the Midwest with her husband and their sassy house rabbit. Learn more about her at marischuh.com.